FREE BONUS

You've made a wonderful choice to pick up this book. Because of this I want to provide you extra resources, insights, and surprises as you journey to becoming the best version of yourself possible.

Just go here…

www.mikejtoy.com/freebook

Nothing excites me more than your success. Looking forward to connecting with you!

THE MAGIC *of* CUSTOMER SERVICE

How the Best Companies Keep Everybody Happy

MIKE TOY

"Doing something and doing it right are two different things. In Mike Toy's book *The Magic of Customer Service*, you will learn this important lesson. Doing things right is a choice. You can decide to be average, good or great. The path to greatness is to understand, everything matters. You have to know more if you want to be more and do more. Learn from Mike and create a mindset of excellence in all areas of your life. You will be glad you did."

—Lee Cockerell, Executive Vice President (Retired and Inspired) Walt Disney World® Resort and Best Selling Author, Creating Magic…Ten Common Sense Leadership Strategies from a Life at Disney, The Customer Rules, Time Management Magic, Career Magic and award winning podcast, Creating Disney Magic.

"Mike Toy helps leaders understand the connection between culture and brand and employee experience and customer experience. In every instance, it's about people and Mike gives practical and easily implemented suggestions to win the hearts of employees and customers!"

—Dee Ann Turner, former Chick-fil-A Vice President and author of Bet on Talent

"Mike Toy's real world observations and fascinating perspective will help you and your people grow!"

—Shep Hyken, New York Times bestselling author of The Cult of the Customer

"With delightful writing and practical tools, Mike Toy keeps customers and culture at the top of your mind. Apply what you learn for an exceptional ride to the top!"

—Ron Kaufman, New York Times bestselling author of Uplifting Service

"Mike Toy knows what it takes for organizations to be the brand customers cannot live without and he details exactly how you can do this in his book."

—John R. DiJulius III, author of The Relationship Economy

"Mike Toy's sharp observations about root problems along with actionable solutions makes this a one-two knockout!"

—Jonah Berger, New York Times bestselling author of Contagious

"Mike Toy gives you the motivational tools you need to boost and strengthen all those around you."

—Brian Tracy, New York Times bestselling author of Eat That Frog

"Want amazing? Count on Mike Toy to help your people develop the attitude and mindset of winners!"

—*Marshall Goldsmith, New York Times #1 bestselling author of Triggers, Mojo, and What Got You Here Won't Get You There*

"Mike Toy knows that culture is key, and a team's success depends on people's mindsets and beliefs in it."

—*Damon West, keynote speaker, bestselling co-author of The Coffee Bean, and author of The Change Agent.*

"Mike Toy gives excellent strategies for any company that wants to create a competitive advantage through astounding customer service."

—*Dr. Tony Alessandra, author of The Platinum Rule for DISC Sales Mastery and The Platinum Rule for Small Business Mastery*

"If you're looking to create a winning culture that's the envy of others, Mike Toy's your guy!"

— *Verne Harnish, Founder Entrepreneurs' Organization (EO) and author of Scaling Up (Rockefeller Habits 2.0)*

"Refreshing and inspiring. Mike Toy has done it again!"

—*Joe Hart, President/CEO of Dale Carnegie*

"If you are looking for the definitive roadmap to create and grow your organization (the kind that will differentiate you from the competition)—look no further. What are you waiting for?"

"Mike takes a comprehensive look at the proven records of great business and institutional leaders, and breaks down crucial components to their success. In the case of Chick-fil-A, he effectively identifies the link between leadership's focus on purpose and how it ultimately impacts the guests' experience."

"Mike Toy's profound wisdom gleaned from some of the greatest leaders and lessons from history is well worth your time. I highly recommend him!"

"From the front line of organizations to the very top, Mike has done his homework. His solutions are a slam dunk!"

"Mike Toy really gets it. His books are jammed pack with actionable ideas that allow business owners to take action immediately outpacing their competition and resulting in great success through increased customer satisfaction and profits. His books are a reference guide to business success!"

"Filled with practical applications, Mike's work will help leaders re-calibrate their business compass."

"This cologne is perfect for your next performance review.
It smells like happy customers!"

For Beano

The more you eat… the more you grow

CONTENTS

PREFACE

A few years ago on my mom's birthday I took her to a San Francisco restaurant to eat dumplings. When we got there the hostess didn't seem happy to be working that day. You can tell on her face. She made minimal eye contact, didn't smile, and didn't even say, "Welcome!"

After we were seated, crusty menus were haphazardly thrown down on our table by the waiter who also didn't greet us either. It was then that I knew the kind of experience I should be expecting the rest of the night so I lowered my expectations.

After the food arrived and we chowed down, I asked for the check, thinking we can finally leave for this unpleasant experience, but I was wrong. We were overcharged for our food so I told the waiter about the situation. He did not apologize. Rather, he gave me a look like "Omigosh, I already have so much to do and you're making me work even harder. Are you serious?" Then he said, "There's nothing I can do about it."

I was shocked as to what he meant. So he begrudgingly explained that his job was to give checks and collect payment, but he wasn't responsible for any price errors or adjustments. I assured him that I wasn't accusing him of overcharging me on purpose and was sure it was a mistake. I told him that maybe he can ask his manager to fix the price.

His eyes widened in an uncomfortable way almost as if he didn't want to ask his boss. Maybe they had a bad relationship. Who knows?

After what seemed to be an eternity, the manager comes to my table and hands me the menu saying, "Check the prices yourself." I was flabbergasted that I was asked to "work". When I pointed out the error, he didn't thank me or apologize. Instead, he had an expression of "Whatever!"

Needless to say, I felt terrible that my dear mother on her birthday had to experience such lousy service.

As I reflect upon that evening, it dawned on me that the heart of customer service isn't do this or don't do this, say this or don't say this. All of that has its place, of course. But the reason why I care about customer service is because I care about my mother. Whether she is at a store or at a gas station or talking to someone on Amazon I want her to feel appreciated, special, cared for, looked after, valued, wherever she is. I want her to have a nice day. My mother has sacrificed so much for me and poured out her love to so many over the years. I'm sure you'd want the same treatment for your mother.

Well, do you watch out for your customers as you would want someone to watch out for your mom? Does your staff do the same? At the heart of all this is, how do you view customers? A necessary evil? A nuisance? Or when you see your customer, do you see your mother? Now that person might not be related to you, but that person is someone's mother (or loved one). Now all we need to do is extend that view of hospitality to others as you would want someone to do for your mom.

In these following pages I share with you the ideas and techniques some of the best companies have employed to keep their customers happy, even in businesses where you may never physically meet the customer.

Thank you for buying this book and supporting my endeavors of making life happier for our community and world.

Mike Toy

INTRODUCTION

Before diving in I want to define customer service as a subset of customer experience. Often times, we think of customer service as how easy it is to return a product or how long we have to wait on hold for the operator or if the wait staff was friendly. Customer experience can certainly include all that, but it can also include how easy it is to navigate your website or being notified of each step of when your package should be arriving. In other words, it's the total experience a customer has from the moment he thinks about your brand or logo.

We once lived in the business culture of "under-promise and over-deliver." The culture has now shifted to "promise boldly and delivery precisely." People want to get the most for their money. They want to know exactly what you will do for them. And they will expect exactly what you promised them. And they want that service or product delivered to them with excellent customer service.

Good customer service is the core of any good business. Without it, you'll have trouble getting clients and keeping clients. After all, if people feel that your company doesn't care about them — their needs, concerns, or questions — it is easier than ever to take their business elsewhere. And since it can usually be done with little effort, they will be quick to do so. Perhaps even worse, they won't hesitate to share their negative experience online and in conversations with friends and family.

The numbers prove it. One survey found that, after just one bad experience with a business, 51% of respondents said they would never choose to interact with the company again. This statistic alone is enough to make any business owner rethink their approach to customer service and support.

Interestingly, though, some businesses feel exempt from expectations of good service. They know that they need to offer good service to their customers, but they often don't see themselves as being in the "people" business. This is especially true with online companies that don't have a physical location or providers who may not have direct or frequent dealings with their clients other than orders that come to them from the web.

However, the fact is simple: Every business is in the "people" business regardless of what kind of business it is. You may not interact with your customers regularly and you may never see them face-to-face, but you still need to know how to respond to their requests and engage them with your brand in a timely, friendly, and effective manner.

Now, if you're thinking that this is easier said than done, you'd be right. Customer service is an art form — one that has taken even the largest brands (with billions of dollars to back their research) decades to perfect. And, no one has yet reached a state of "ideal" customer service.

As time goes on, your brand will change. Your products will change. And your customers' needs will change leading to ever-changing requirements for customer service. That makes it hard to capture the little nuances that make for good service, but all customer service should begin with the same principles.

These are the foundational principles that every big brand out there utilizes in order to keep customers happy. Each brand then puts its own twist on things to help build a lasting relationship with their customer base and keep them coming back. Whether your company is a scrappy upstart or a time-tested titan, customer service will frame your success or spell your doom.

Customer service is more than just a department. It's an integral part of your brand and business. It's a way of viewing people. If you view people as a nuisance or an annoyance, no matter how much training one has, it will show up in the work that is presented to them.

But on the other hand, if you treat customers the way you'd want someone to treat your mom (better yet, your grandmother), you'll be glad they came by to give your products and services a try. Customers are the reason why any business or company survives. It's why anyone has a job.

I think customer service is best understood when you focus on providing a good customer experience overall. The customer's experience is the sum total of how they interact with your brand. It includes not just the moment when a customer walks into the building, but his/her experience with your brand before and after that, as well.

In any case, no matter the industry you work in, without good customer service, there's no way your company will see sustainable sales. Even if your product or service is excellent, even if what you offer is unique and you are "the only game in town," today's customer will find a way to avoid you if you leave them frustrated.

In this guide, we'll explore the ways that different companies—from Chick-fil-A to Amazon—are using customer service to not only address concerns and problems, but also stand out from their competitors in a way that makes their brand more personable, more approachable, and ultimately more worthy of people's business.

Let's begin!

CHAPTER 1
APPEAL TO THE SENSES

Imagine you walked into a storefront and found the following: the lights were dim, the entryway was dirty, the carpets were undusted, the trash cans were filled, and there were boxes in the aisle blocking the walkway. Would you really want to shop there? The average person would turn on their heels and leave, swearing never to come back. After all, whether they're disorganized shelves or dirty floors, it wouldn't make for a very enticing shopping experience.

Such a storefront would probably give you a pretty negative view of the brand overall, too. If they don't seem to care how their storefront looks, do they really care about the quality of their product? Would they care if you had an issue with your purchase or needed help? Most people would confidently (and correctly) wager—no.

The same is true for restaurants. No matter how expensive the restaurant's fare, no matter how impressed you are with the valet parking service, and no matter how renowned the chef, when you are seated at a dirty table, or you find crumbs on the chair, or are handed a sticky menu with the residue of food, you wonder about the condition of the kitchen where your food will be cooked.

The way your company appears to the random customer walking in says more than you'd expect about your brand. Customers form first impressions about businesses in the same way people do with other people. In similar fashion, first impressions are lasting and tough to escape.

Mystery shopping companies often have their team members visit stores and evaluate all of the sensory information:

- How bright is it?
- How does it smell?
- Are the trash cans emptied?
- Are all of the lights on the signage lit?
- Are the doors and windows free of smudges?
- Is the music too loud?
- Are the restrooms cleaned, stocked, and fresh-smelling, etc?

How can we solve the first impression problem? If you have a physical location, approach it the way a brand new customer would. How easy it is for customers to pull in to your parking lot from the street? Is there parking? It parking expensive? Are parking spots so close together that it is a hazard to back in or pull out? How far does a customer have to walk to reach his or her car?

A swanky retail district in the Main Line section of Philadelphia, Pennsylvania offers the finest specialty stores in the world. There are no Burger King's or McDonald's in this part of town. There's not even a Starbuck's. Rather, it is peppered with epicurean coffee houses, swanky art dealers, and one-of-a-kind gourmet eateries. It's the "high-rent district" to be sure. But the parking is something akin to "Nightmare on Elm Street." For starters, there is only one parking lot in the center of town. And it ain't free. It's not even cheap. Each spot is metered by the hour. The sparse on-street parking is metered as well. Worse, the parking lanes in both locations are so close together or so strangely angled, there are frequent "fender-benders" when shaky drivers misjudge their entry or exit.

The problem, if it isn't already obvious, is that often, cars pull into the area, drive around for several minutes, and then drive away. One can't be sure, but it seems they gave up in search of other places to spend their money. Many are the unfortunate people who buy a large piece of art and then have the task of lugging it several blocks to their vehicles. And customers don't have the luxury of browsing at the leisure for fear that they will overstay the time on their parking meter. Shockingly, these business owners take the chance of letting customers leave their stores to feed their meters and risk the possibility that they will either decide to go home or see another store they'd rather shop in.

> **PRO TIP:** Never give your customers a reason
> to leave your store. The research proves
> that longer they stay, the more they buy.

The fix? There is a huge empty lot just a mile and a half away. The shop owners could simply petition the city to convert the parking lanes into valet lanes. The shop owners could pitch in on the cost of free valet service, which would be very much in keeping with their tenor of the region. It would increase traffic, lengthen the stay of customers in-store, satisfy a customer frustration, and increase revenues far above the cost of the valet. Add to that the swag-factor of offering valet parking, and you have a recipe for success.

But it's not only brick-and-mortar retailers who seem to have *blind spots* about their appearance and accessibility. Many online retailers fail to evaluate the ease of navigating their websites. E-commerce is a critical component of nearly every business in the world economy. So, why are businesses so painfully unaware of their poor online appearance?

Amazon.com continues to top the chart in e-commerce sales. On the other hand, Walmart, which enjoys the position of #2 in retail sales in the U. S. is struggling to dominate online. Walmart's sales as of 2019 represent only 5% of its overall sales.

In a Vox.com article, Jason Del Ray writes:

> *This is the reality. Lore is still struggling to get Walmart's entire executive team and board to accept, though sources say McMillon also acknowledges it: E-commerce in the US is becoming a "winner take all" industry. Or, at a minimum, a "winner take most" market.*

So, why is it that so many businesses today continue to accept customers onto a website that isn't appealing to the eye? These days, many people who see your website won't ever actually go to your physical location—if you even have one—and that means it is often the first point of contact. How is it representing your company?

Your website is likely your first opportunity to display your company's excellent (or shoddy) customer service philosophy.

You also need to think about other aspects of your brand and the things customers come in contact with. Whether it's the lawn out front your bakery, the packaging of your beauty products, or any other visual, it needs to be appealing.

CASE STUDY: DISNEY

Disney is known as the happiest place on earth, and its staff (or "cast members") certainly bring the magic when they arrive each day. In fact, I just love how Disney refers to every team member as a cast member, helping to instantly get everyone in the mindset that they aren't simply working a shift—they are taking on a meaningful role at the park.

And, like most people who have gone to Disney, I have great respect and appreciation for such cast members. I vividly remember my first time going to Disneyland when I was about five years old. I was immensely impressed by how clean the park was. Everything was absolutely perfect.

Disney goes above and beyond regarding keeping things appealing to the senses. There are near endless examples of this attention to pleasing the customer, including how they design the park, the colors they use, and the songs that are played over the sound system.

After all, just to keep with the flow and magic, cast members use a secret tunnel system *underneath* the park just so they are never seen out of costume or out of character. The characters also take the tunnels to get to and from meet-and-greets so that you don't run into a character in a themed area where they shouldn't be. So, you'll never see Snow White going through Frontierland.

They also paint walls and trash cans so that they don't become eyesores. They make sure cast members wear their best outfits and their best smiles. And, they instill great values in each member of the cast. You'll never see clutter or trash in Disney because cast members are trained to constantly look for things to tidy as they go about their daily tasks.

Plus, cast members are even trained on *how* to pick up trash. Rather than simply bending over, they are trained to do it in a sweeping motion that keeps with the general theme and happy feelings of the magical world Disney has created.

Over 44,000 guests go in and out of Disney every single day, can you imagine the amount of trash they create? Disney's approach requires not only designated custodial workers, but they have trained *thousands* of cast members to pitch in and help, which definitely takes a load off the janitors and keeps the park in tip-top shape.

Disney is so obsessed with "appearances," even their corporate headquarters, which their guests will likely never see, had to be more than just a typical office building. The design of their Orlando headquarters was done by Arata Isozak and won the 2019 Pritzker Prize for architecture.

So why do companies allow the physical and virtual locations to appear outdated and/or run-down?

"Do you have any other collateral...
besides this e-mail from a Nigerian prince?"

CHAPTER 2
ANTICIPATE NEEDS

Anticipating a customer's needs is a major part of good customer service. There are many different ways to anticipate the needs of customers, and it will vary depending on the types of products or services you sell.

To get started, think about the average person who walks through your doors. What are they coming in for and what can you do to improve their experience? Hotels are a fantastic example in the service industry as there is a lot the check-in staff can do to improve a guest's experience before they even see their room.

Think about it: If you walk into a hotel, most likely after getting off a long flight, what are some things you always want to be ready? Hotels already standardize shampoo, conditioner, and other basic toiletries so you don't have to worry about digging out or purchasing your own. However, beyond that, they can also go the extra mile at the check-in desk to further personalize your experience.

Having a luggage cart at the ready for large families, for instance, can do wonders for relieving tired arms after a long trip. Even something so simple as offering champagne to a couple who appears to be escaping on a short weekend trip or pointing out the lobby's market or snack bar to a family with young kids can certainly start improving their stay right away.

CASE STUDY: HILTON

Anticipating your customer's needs doesn't begin or end with how you market or describe your products. As in the case of Hilton and other hotels, the hospitality business has anticipation down pat. In fact, any business stands to learn a lot about customer service from businesses in the hospitality industry, and such hotels are no exception.

Take, for example, the check-in staff. I'm a bit of a customer experience fanatic, and I like seeing good service delivered. Whether I was awaiting my room or a ride from the hotel, I've often hung out in the front lobby of the Hilton, pretending to be sitting and checking the news on my phone but often eavesdropping on conversations at the front desk out of boredom.

One time, there was a family with small kids and the Hilton staff anticipated their needs perfectly. When they see a family check-in with young children, they consistently anticipate their needs. They offer roll-away beds for the little ones, if needed, and then provide whatever goodies they may have behind the counter—like cookies or coloring books—to keep the kids happy while the check-in process is completed, and the parents settle into their rooms.

Similarly, I've seen check-in staff anticipate the needs of couples. When the hotel check-in desk has a couple's special reservation on file, they can help anticipate their needs by offering suggestions for local restaurants, activities, and places to go. At an up-scale location, the check-in staff often has a special gift basket or complimentary wine awaiting the couple when they arrive in their room.

It's these little things that make customers remember you.

Josh Brown, Content and Community Manager at Fieldboom, writes:

> *Providing fluffy add-ons is not the same as added value. Virgin Atlantic added amenities such as TV sets and Wi-Fi to their flights over the years… In-flight entertainment has been in-demand since commercial flight became routine; Virgin just figured out a way to up the ante by including individual TVs in all headrests. Virgin knows many of its passengers are businessmen and women who need to stay connected to the grid at all times—even at 35,000 feet. So, by providing Wi-Fi to passengers, they responded to a need. Both of these amenities are now par-for-the-course which brings up a point…*

> *Exceeding expectations is an ongoing, cyclical process. When you exceed your customer's expectations, you provide something they didn't expect.*

> *But, once you provide such added value, your customers will come to expect it—meaning you'll have to find new ways to "wow" them.*

It's all about your viewpoint. Successful leaders know that their organizations have to be looked at from multiple perspectives:

1. From the perspective of the customer – Customers are more demanding now than ever. They don't just expect you to meet their expectations. They expect you to exceed them. In fact, they expect you to anticipate them. Companies need to know the customer's need before the customer is even aware of the need themselves. And when customers are put in the untenable position of telling you their needs, you had better be ready to respond instantly. Responding to a customer's complaint in the moment is fine. But it is not enough. Companies need to be able to identify what gave rise to the complaint and put systems in place to address every possible future complaint of its kind. There is also the issue of the viability of your product or service. Is your product a necessity or a luxury?

2. From the perspective of the team member – How team members see your business is a critical limiter to the level of customer service. Team members should have a positive outlook on the company and see their own future within it. We have all experienced team members who are disgruntled and the damper they put on our buying experience. In a recent Forbes magazine issue, contributor Cheryl Conner writes: "What effect can a disgruntled employee have in your office? People frequently underestimate the power of the 'pissed off.' The topic has captured

some significant attention in my recent column for Harvard Business Review: Are you Creating Disgruntled Employees? In general, disgruntled employees have been known to: (1) Create irreversible damage to your brand, (2) Alienate your most valuable clients and cause very expensive mistakes, (3) Leak important company information and participate in internet "bad-mouthing" (4) Stop potential hires from joining the company (5) Cause others around them to be upset and disengaged in their work (6) Be guilty of theft, tardiness, missed deadlines, etc. In other words, disgruntled employees are harmful to any organization"

3. From the perspective of the leader – Perhaps the most important factor in great customer service is the leader's perspective of the company and customer. Leaders need to know exactly who their customers are and what they want. As we've already seen, failure to know who your customers are and what business you're in means you will be offering the right service to the wrong people or worse—the wrong service to the right people. Either way, it's a recipe for a quick "Out of Business" sign on the front door. Leaders need to know everything about their customer psychographically. Startup leaders do a fantastic job of concentrating on the customer. They think about the end-user experience. They think about every step of the customer's interaction with their company. They fuss over locations, lobbies, aisle-width, websites, color schemes, etc. But as the business grows, the focus quietly shifts to stock prices, reports, etc. and the customer is lost in the shuffle.

It's all about perspective.

How does your customer like to shop?

While it's not yet time to seal the coffin on shopping malls and bank buildings, the trend away from brick-and-mortar cannot be denied. Is your business better suited for a physical location, a purely virtual presence, or some combination of the two? Contributor Greg Maloney of Forbes magazine writes:

> *Online sales from brick-and-mortar retailers (e.g. Target) were more than half that of pure-play e-commerce retailers in 2017 (pure-play: $261.9 billion vs. brick and mortar: $179.9 billion). Meaning, we are truly seeing a blending of the channels and a realization from retailers that to properly compete they need to have a presence everywhere, online and off.*

Do they shop online, or do they enjoy visiting brick-and-mortar stores? Do they make spontaneous purchases, or are they more conscious about their spending?

Once you know the answers to these questions, you'll be in a much better position to provide a solution to your customers' problems that will exceed their expectations in all areas. When you are intentional about your customer's needs and carefully analyze their buying habits, you can meet their expectations and you ensure they return to your company again and again.

CHAPTER 3
GO THE EXTRA MILE

As HubSpot puts it: "Customer service is a company's opportunity to connect with customers, solve problems, and show they care. And when customer service is executed well, it can resonate with customers for years to come." After all, at the end of the day, no customer is going to remember your marketing or branding if your customer service isn't up-to-par.

"THE CUSTOMER IS ALWAYS RIGHT"

It's a saying seemingly as old as business itself, and there's good reason for it. While the customer might not always be right in your eyes, taking this approach means you are committing to a few things as a business:

- You will never argue with customers over a problem, or over whether or not a "problem" is actually a problem.
- You will always strive to make customers happy, even (and especially) when they have exceedingly high commands.
- Your business will put customers and their satisfaction first, no matter what.

These are tough promises to make and keep, but for companies that actually follow through, the levels of customer satisfaction and loyalty are simply unmatched.

ALWAYS STRIVE TO DO MORE AND BE BETTER

An article from Entrepreneur helps summarize why going the extra mile matters, and how to do it well:

> *"This "spirit of excellence" mindset is apparent in the case of one of my mentors, the extraordinary Napoleon Hill. Hill utilized what he called the QQMA formula in his everyday life that pushed him to go the extra mile in any endeavor. QQMA stands for the quality of service you render, the quantity of service you render, plus the mental attitude with which you render the service. Hill put an intention on each aspect of the service he provided and strove for excellence in delivering that service, in terms of quality, quantity and his attitude."*

If you need an easy way to member it, just think: QQMA. That's Quality, Quantity, and Mental Attitude related to the service you're delivering.

Some good "rules of thumb" that fall under the category of going the extra mile are simple and straightforward, but still worth mentioning (and emphasizing) on a daily basis. Avoiding conflict and doing everything you can to resolve customer conflict is a major point of focus for any successful company. Just take these examples into consideration.

CASE STUDY: CHICK-FIL-A

I love Chick fil-A! When I'm having a not-so-stellar day and need a quick pick-me-up I visit a Chick fil-A. It's not just because I'm always in the mood for a delicious chicken sandwich-it's to have the pleasure of seeing people who are happy to see me and determined to make my day brighter.

Training your team members to simply "be nice" goes a very long way. Chick-fil-A is an excellent company to showcase in that regard, constantly and consistently making the news for team members who truly do go the extra mile.

The company that reportedly earns double the revenue of McDonald's, even though they always close on Sundays, knows a thing or two about customer service—and it's no secret that their service is how they recently climbed to the top of the list, dethroning In-and-Out as America's favorite restaurant. According to Business Insider, it's "the most profitable fast-food chain in

America on a per-location basis." The same article declared that "Chick-fil-A has been ranked #1 in politeness of staff."

Part of what makes Chick-fil-A so successful is their strict requirements. Not just anyone can open a Chick-fil-A. Just read this paragraph from the company's website: "Chick-fil-A operators must successfully complete an extensive, multi-week training program prior to taking over operation of a franchised Chick-fil-A restaurant business. With additional development courses and franchise support available, Chick-fil-A operators are equipped to handle decisions and reap the rewards of a challenging business."

One recent article sums the brand's reputation up perfectly, with a piece titled: "Another Chick-fil-A Worker Turns into Good Samaritan, Going Above and Beyond for WW II Veteran." The article pulls in just a few examples of the amazing feats of Chick-fil-A workers from recent months, highlighting:

- **Southern Hospitality:** The time when Chick-fil-A sent sandwiches to stranded drivers during a freak snowstorm that affected traffic across Georgia and Alabama.

- **Jet Ski Rescues:** The time when an elderly couple stranded in the floods called Chick-fil-A to order a rescue boat, a request to which the manager's husband quickly responded to, heading to the Houston home of the two frequent customers on the back of a jet ski.

- **Helping Hands:** Recently, Chick-fil-A workers handed out free food and water to workers at the Southaven Walmart following violent crime that left them stranded outside as local businesses went on lockdown.

By far, Chick-fil-A remains one of the top examples of putting customers and community first, and it has certainly paid off.

CASE STUDY: SOUTHWEST AIRLINES

There's a reason why Southwest is ranked one of the top airlines in the industry. They make things easy. You'll appreciate Southwest more once you fly other airlines. At Southwest, there are no change fees. So if you happen to want a later or earlier flight just cancel your current flight and you'll get your entire credit back to be applied to another flight of your choice. How cool is that!

Another reason why customers love Southwest is because they allow two checked bags to fly free. This, too, is virtually unheard of in the industry. Many airlines will charge you at least $50 for each checked bag. This makes flying Southwest a no-brainer.

So just here are two excellent reasons why customers would prefer to fly Southwest. But there's more. Southwest flight attendants are happy to see you. When the airline first got started many of the flight attendants were cheerleaders so there was a positive company culture vibe. It still goes on today.

After you get your drinks, flight attendant will come around again and ask, "Can I get you anything else?" Now, flight attendants certainly don't "have to" do this. But this memorable gesture just communicates to customers that they are happy to serve.

If you ever call Southwest their customer service reps are equally positive. I've had numerous issues over the years where I had to call them to fix from accidentally cancelling the wrong flights to seeing if I could get the lower priced fare that just went up a minute ago and they were always more than happy to help me out.

There was once when Southwest lost my luggage. Fortunately, it was found the next day. They offered to ship my luggage to my house, but since I needed it right away I went to the airport to pick it up. To compensate me for the trouble, they gave me a $50 voucher without me having to ask.

On another occasion, while waiting for my flight at the gate, Southwest offered vouchers for customers who win at the bean bag toss game. I was thrilled to have won a $50 voucher.

These are excellent examples of how "going the extra mile" will equate to customer loyalty. Now, unless Southwest doesn't fly to where I need to go, it's my default airline to travel domestically.

Despite having been exposed to years of advertising for Southwest, this experience is what convinced me to be a loyal customer, which reflects HubSpot's statement: "Customer support shouldn't be an afterthought. Happy customers come from excellent service and are your best advocates—even better than your most talented marketers."

"Who picked 'I Can't Get No Satisfaction'
to be our on-hold music?"

CHAPTER 4
INSTILL A STRONG COMPANY IMAGE

Another formula that your business must follow surrounds the image your team members help build for your brand. At the end of the day, no matter how strong you think your branding is whether online or in store, it's your team members and the way they present themselves that will determine how customers experience your brand.

> *"Any employee that interacts and deals with customers is eligible for customer service training. And given how your customers are your best growth opportunity, each and every employee should be working hard to keep them happy—whether from the position of marketer, receptionist, or customer service representative."* (HubSpot, 2019)

Forbes explained why in an article from 2016, which opened with: "Brand image is more than a logo that identifies your business, product or service. Today, it is a mix of the associations consumers make based on every interaction they have with your business. Most entrepreneurs and small business owners don't really think about their brand image until there's a problem with the image they're developing."

Even if team members address customers with the right branded messaging and even if they wear a smile when your customers are in front of them, smaller things can make a big impact on how people think about your company. For instance, team members should never be permitted to smoke when wearing company uniforms.

This rule is very important to enforce, because not only does the image of a smoking team member impact your brand, the lingering odor will also impact the entire environment in which other team members and customers spend their time.

Likewise, you should always make sure that team members are taking proper care of their uniforms and that they are always wearing their uniforms when working. Even small things, like name tags, can go a long way in helping customers recognize and be more comfortable interacting with your workers. In turn, these things will help workers provide better service while building your brand.

Instilling the idea in your team members that they are constantly "building the brand" any time they wear your uniform is going to help them be more mindful of their actions. However, beyond simply telling them that they are part of your company's brand when in uniform, you also need to tell them what that means and make sure that managers are demonstrating that meaning through their own actions.

In other words, managers need to lead by example and consistently showcase the quality of service you want every team member to provide. The way customers perceive your brand ultimately comes down to how they perceive your team members, so don't underestimate the importance of training them in this regard.

So, remind team members that representing your brand goes beyond acting a certain way. Customers will see more team members than they will talk to, which is why every team member should be seen being productive and working with a smile. They should be quick to greet customers and say hello and they should always "look the part" when in a customer's view.

That means a big smile, properly groomed hair, clothes that are wrinkle-free, shiny shoes, and fresh breath. They need to take good care of themselves and come into work with pride each and every day, and customers will notice it even if they don't have a conversation with them. There will be a different attitude that permeates the environment and a happy energy that encourages customers to return.

Above all, you need to teach your team members about instilling positivity in customers. Everyone has bad days, and you should recognize that, but make sure team members know to never show negativity to customers.

However, they should know that there are open lines of communication and that they can turn to their supervisor to speak openly about issues—as long as they know to keep internal issues internal and *never* take their problems out on paying customers.

When you show your team members that you are around to listen and that you care about their experience just as much as they care about the customer's experience, they will represent your brand in a very positive light.

CASE STUDY: APPLE

I own and use multiple Apple products and, chances are, you have used one in the past, too. Apple has one of the strongest brands in the world. Not only do their products have people rushing to the stores days before new products hit the shelves just so they can be the first to get their hands on stuff—they also consistently present a strong brand image through their uniform store design and impressive customer service.

While the company as a whole displays an image of quality and innovation, individual stores further reinforce that image through highly-trained sales staff who know the products inside and out. But, one thing that I am always impressed by when I enter into an Apple store is how non-pushy the sales staff are. I go into a lot of high-end or "luxury" brand stores and the sales staff are usually quick to jump on a potential client. It's akin to walking into a dealership's lot and feeling swarmed by sales reps within minutes of your arrival.

Apple stores, however, are always different. There's no competitiveness amongst team members who are racing to make commission on a big sale. Rather, a person will kindly approach you to ask how they can help—and then they will genuinely do their best to assist in any way they can. Behind those sharp-looking uniforms are great people who really know their stuff. They greet you as soon as you arrive and then sincerely work to understand what they can do for you.

If you're in there to buy a product, they won't just try to get you to buy the most expensive thing they can sell to you. I have seen it for myself and others on many occasions that, even if you come in thinking about the newest, hottest, most expensive product, they are going to narrow your wants and needs down to key features and try to help you understand which products can fulfill those wants and needs.

So, maybe you'll walk in there wanting to try out the newest iPhone, and after they let you use it for a while and try out all the different features, you decide it's not what you need after all. You won't feel any pressure from the sales staff to get it anyway. Instead, they'll gladly take the time to show you other products that will work better for you.

Likewise, whenever I go in when I'm having a problem with one of their products, I can walk right up to the Genius Bar and they'll help me get it sorted out. For instance, I took my iPhone there recently because I was having issues, and the guy there was so knowledgeable, I was out of there in under 10 minutes. In that instance, it was a simple case of user error and I left with new knowledge of the product.

I can't recall the countless times I've done this and I've never left there unsatisfied. Even when issues can't be resolved immediately at the counter, the entire service experience leaves you feeling like you have been listened to, understood, and taken care of—and that's what excellent customer service is all about.

The point is, at an Apple store, every team member acts as a brand advocate. Not only do these team members truly know and love the products they are selling, they're also huge fans of Apple and its company culture as a whole. And, through their work, they help to turn everyone who walks into an Apple store into a lover of the brand as well—and that's why Apple has such incredible high brand loyalty and extremely high brand recognition around the world.

It's a great test for your company. Are your team members also customers of your store? When they're not working, are they buying, using, and talking about the brand? If not, perhaps the first sales presentation you need to make is in-house!

CHAPTER 5
BE AN EXPERT

If there is one thing that your workers should receive, it's on-going training. If you do not yet know the importance of on-going training, you could be missing out on a huge opportunity.

On-going training helps turn your team members into experts that will ultimately be able to sell your products to more people. Training is able to do this by always preparing your team members to answer the tough questions that customers will lob at them.

Being a product expert isn't just important for typical sales positions, either. Every team member can benefit from knowing your brand, your products, and your customers better.

If you own a clothing store, for instance, your team members should be well-trained in being able to identify sizing for customers. If you own a pet store, your team members should know the basics of pet care and be able to offer good guidelines for any new animal a customer may be taking home.

The list goes on. Regardless of what you are selling, your team members need to know why they are selling it and who they are selling it to. This goes back to knowing your customer personas, or the types of people who walk into your store. When your team members can identify the types of customers they deal with, they'll be able to help each one much more effectively.

A simple formula for business success is two-fold:
1. Train, train, train
2. Inspect what you expect

The importance of training cannot be overstated. When customers interact with your team members, they don't see them as individuals apart from your company. Your team members <u>are</u> your company. So when a customer asks a question, they expect your team member to know the answer. In those rare cases when they don't, the path to getting the right answer should be easy and fast.

Implementing a training program is fairly easy. Of course, team members need to be trained for their roles. But are there other areas of knowledge we might explore? For example, do all of your team members know the history of the founding of your company? Can they speak about it accurately and with pride? Imagine the impact on a customer when they ask, "By the way, how long has this store been in business?" and they hear a frontline team member passionately tell the story. Let's face it, every business has a great back story. Businesses are not dropped out of the sky by "corporate fairies." Every business is born out of struggle and pain, which always makes for a great story. So offer training every year that includes discussion of the history of the company.

Training should also include customer service strategies. Books, like this one, can be used to enhance a team member's knowledge base. For example, discussions about conflict resolution strategies can help team members better handle customer complaints.

Studies show that an ongoing culture of training:
- Increases morale
- Improves retention
- Improves areas of weakness
- Enhances customer service

Inspecting what you expect is simply checking to ensure that the training you have done is achieving the results you intended.

CASE STUDY: HOME IMPROVEMENT

Up to this point, all of the case studies have been very positive. However, I would like to explain an example that I have personally witnessed that demonstrates what happens when team members *aren't* experts on what they are selling.

When visiting a home improvement store recently, I asked a team member to help me find a particular type of wire for a project I was working on back at home. They seemed nice enough and were quick to point me to Aisle 7, but when I arrived on Aisle 7, I still couldn't locate what I was looking for.

The aisle had chains and different ropes that could be cut to length, but not the wire I was in search of. But, while growing a bit frustrated, another team member walked by just as I realized the issue. I asked them where to find it, assuming that surely they'd know. They sent me to Aisle 11 and continued on with whatever they were doing.

Of course, when I got to Aisle 11, the wire wasn't there either. So, I asked yet another team member, hoping maybe the third time was the charm, as they say. Unfortunately, that's when that team member informed me they didn't actually carry the wire I was looking for.

Had the first team member told me that, I could have been out the door and onto another location in a matter of minutes. Instead, I spent well over half an hour going back and forth with team members who thought they knew what I needed or half-listened to my request or perhaps made up an aisle number all together just to get me out of their hair. In fact, I'm still not entirely convinced that the store didn't have the wire I needed because the staff seemed to have no clue what was where.

While I may wander back into that store if it's convenient and I already know where to find what I'm after, I will never go out of my way to give them my business. If a competitor is closer, easier, or seems friendlier, I'll take my business there.

In reality, the few times I have been back to this store since that experience, I have constantly been reminded of the careless, seemingly clueless staff that couldn't help me—and that's doing terrible things for the company's overall brand.

That's another reason why this experience was worth sharing; it demonstrates how important (and difficult) it is to hire the right staff, especially when managing multiple locations or working through franchises.

The parent company has to keep close tabs on their locations and the management at each location to help avoid bad customer experiences like the one I had. It also proves that consistent, continual, on-going training is essential because it's not that anyone was particularly rude, they just didn't know what they should, and that cost me a lot of time and them a *lot* of business.

But imagine if the team member actually walked the customer to the right aisle. And, beyond that, as they're walking, he asks them why they're looking for that particular screw or tool and they tell him that they're building a treehouse. Maybe he'd offer a better suggestion, like longer or larger screws for assembly. Beyond that, he might also go on to help them think about other aspects of the project that they may not have considered.

He might say, "Hey, by the way, have you thought about getting a water seal so that the wood doesn't get water damage when it rains? Let me take you over to the water seal aisle. I know just the kind that would be perfect for your project." See the importance of being the expert? When you are, you save people time and frustration, and you'll win their business over and over again because they trust you.

"The bad news is, our customers hate us. The good news is,
we have a lot fewer customers than we used to!"

CHAPTER 6
BACK UP YOUR TEAM MEMBERS

Managers and supervisors should always have their team members' backs, it's as simple as that.

Management is supposed to be there to support the team members, reassure them, tell them when they're doing the right thing and, of course, call them out when they need to do something differently. However, above anything, management needs to work on helping team members feel empowered to do their job the best they can.

I have encountered far too many managers that do not support their staff when it counts. They are quick to blame issues on team members and, when things are going wrong, they might as well be throwing gasoline into the fire. Rather than helping workers see the light at the end of the tunnel, bad managers chastise them for falling behind, not moving fast enough, forgetting things, or just for having not solved the problems that management should be solving instead.

Good management means:
- Recognizing and mitigating issues in a way that empowers staff members to do the best they can;
- Supporting the frontline who are trying hard and showing appreciation for those who align with the company's values;
- Encouraging workers to do more, rather than ridiculing them for not doing enough;
- Building a team morale where everyone supports each other and helps pick up the slack for more even work distribution.

If the management at your business is not actively in a supportive role that keeps teams aligned and individual workers on track, you're managing your business wrong. That might sound harsh, but it's the simple truth.

Backing your frontline takes on several forms:

TRAINING

We'll talk more about training later. However, it is important to note here that training is critical to ensure team members have a full toolkit they can use to service customers.

SUPPORT

Team members almost always bring their problems to work. When a team member is suffering from a death, divorce or financial hardship, it's tough for that team member to deliver stellar customer service. Offering some sort of team member support system, helps team members feel that they have help with the struggles of their lives, but also helps them release their concerns so they can take care of your customers.

CLEAR EXPECTATIONS

The hardest obstacle for a team member to overcome is your failure to set clear expectations. Every team member should have a written, well-defined job description and be evaluated on at least a yearly basis. Day-to-day, managers need to clearly communicate what they need and check for understanding.

TAKING THE BLAME

If team members are following your instructions and it results in an unhappy customer, managers can diffuse the situation by taking responsibility to both the team member and the customer. The manager needs to have the ability to say, "I put that rule in place. I can see how it isn't working in this situation. I'm sorry." This diffuses conflict, backs the team member, and lets the customer see your genuineness.

CASE STUDY: P.F. CHANG'S

I can think of countless examples when the managers had to come in and back up the frontline workers. Or, at least, when they *should* have. The service industry (and the food service industry, in particular), certainly has the most.

A recent example comes from P.F. Chang's. If you don't know the name, it's a chain Asian restaurant and I love their food. But, they stay awfully busy. While they normally are able to keep up with the demand pretty well, even through the busiest times of the lunch and dinner hours, I was at one that happened to be understaffed—and everyone noticed.

I am uncertain what happened—maybe a cook didn't show or someone quit or something else, but the kitchen was lagging behind on food orders. The customers were highly demanding, and people like me felt the food would be worth the wait, but the cook staff simply couldn't keep up. Some customers had waited 45 minutes to get their appetizer, and it was getting ridiculous.

Given that I know customer service inside and out, it's in situations like these that I can't help but feel bad for the people behind the counter. After all, they were doing the best they could to get everyone their dinner, but some customers simply weren't having it. After waiting a long time, some customers began complaining to the wait staff in tones that certainly fit the descriptions of aggressive, mean, and hateful.

Of course, it's in these situations that I wish everyone would just realize it's never the wait staff's fault. They want to bring you your food just as much as you want to eat it, but they have no control over what the kitchen is doing or how long they are taking. Still, everyone seemed to be taking their anger out on their waiter or waitress, and I saw many getting visibly upset by the fuss.

As the wait staff grew visibly discouraged by the ridicule, I was about to reach out to our waitress and offer some friendly words when I saw the manager in the corner doing just that. I was proud that the manager had stepped in and was reassuring the wait staff that they were doing the best they could.

I could see the difference that made for the front-of-house. The staff grew more confident and a genuine smile returned to their faces as they realized that the manager had their back and they were doing their best. He did an excellent job boosting the morale of the staff, which ultimately enabled them to keep their act together until the food finally came out.

CHAPTER 7
TAKE COMPLAINTS AS ADVICE

Far too many companies "shut down" when faced with a complaint. In other words, when a customer gets upset or expresses a negative opinion, they practically put their hands over their ears and refuse to hear it. Not only does that make it extremely hard to help turn the experience around for that specific customer, but it also means you're missing out on feedback about a problem that could potentially be a lot bigger.

> *"The average American tells 15 people when they've had a poor customer service experience." (AE)*

It's no secret that when some customers come in and they have a bad experience, it is for reasons beyond your control. Maybe they were having a bad day long before encountering your company. Or, perhaps they were very upset that you didn't have a particular thing in stock on the day they went shopping. Sometimes, they misunderstand what your company is able to do for them. In any case, while it can be hard to do, it's important that your business hears them out and meets their complaints with compassion.

As the saying goes, the customer is always right. That has never been more true in today's self-focused society. The truth is, the customer is often wrong. But, in your eyes and the eyes of your team members, they can never be seen as wrong.

So, when customers are displeased about something, there is no other way to begin fixing them except to hear the customer out regarding what has upset them. Is the price too high? Is the item unavailable? Is the wait too long? Listen to these complaints because, there's a hard truth: More often than not, more people share the complaint than you hear from.

The absolute worst response a company could have to a complaint is, "Well, you're the first person to say anything about it," or anything of the sort. While sometimes customer issues are confined to just that one customer, usually, that complaint can be tied to a bigger systemic issue in your company. Perhaps no one has spoken up about it in the past, but whether you're hearing a complaint for the first time or the hundredth time, you need to listen to it.

You may be surprised just how much value customer complaints can hold. That's because, when you really listen and avoid taking the issue personally, you can leave your emotions out of it. No matter how much you may disagree with the customer, if they genuinely feel a certain way, they are doing you a big favor by telling you about it. After all, do you know how many customers have a bad experience and then leave without ever saying anything at all?

Exterminators will tell you that if you see a bug in your home, there are 100 just like it hiding in the walls and floors. It's an unpleasant analogy, but an effective one. Customer complaints function in a very similar manner. For every loudmouthed, overbearing customer who takes you to task about your failure to satisfy them, there are many more who were equally displeased, but said nothing. They just voted with their feet by leaving your store and silently vowing never to return.

In this sense, you should take customer complaints as not only an opportunity to learn, grow, and improve, but also the chance to try and salvage the relationship. The customer has spoken up and told you what's wrong; that means you could potentially address the problem. Whether or not you do may be decided on case-by-case basis, but at least consider a solution and, at the very least, work to understand what the actual issue is.

GIVE CUSTOMERS A SAFE PLACE TO COMPLAIN

A major mistake many companies make is not giving customers a safe and easy way to voice their concerns. Absent a way to let you know what displeased them, they turn to google reviews, Facebook, Manta, Foursquare, or Yelp for a venue to air their grievances. In more extreme cases, when the customer wants action, they turn to the Better Business Bureau where an advocate will try to help resolve the dispute. Sadly, many business owners are unaware or unconcerned of the damage these review sites are doing to their businesses. And failure to respond to a BBB request will count as a serious strike against a business. The BBB even lists every complaint and notes your failure to respond on their site.

But there are many ways business owners can protect their companies from the onslaught of negative customer complaints and, potentially, win a customer back.

1. Give customers a place to complain – Make it clear both in-store and online how customers can funnel their complaints directly to you. For example, most major car companies will send you an email immediately after your purchase of a new car or visit to their service department to give you a place to let off some steam if you were dissatisfied or shout their praises if you have a great experiences. This is ingenious because once customers have gotten the complaint off their chests, they are less likely to publish their displeasure to the world. One smart store owner posted a sign that read: "If you had a great shopping experience, please tell a manager. If you didn't, please, please, please tell a manager."

2. Take online reviews seriously – Thinking that an online review is buried in cyberspace is a huge mistake. Broadly.com and many others have alleged that "in fact, 84% of people trust online reviews as much as a personal recommendation."

3. Respond to every customer complaint – Online complaints are tough to keep up with, but it is critical to develop a system to do so. The point of responding within the day is two-fold: 1) It helps preserve your relationship with that customer. 2) Every other customer who reads the response will know that you care about your clientele. At least once per day, you or someone on your team must sit down and read the day's reviews on the major sites. Nearly all of them offer a place for you to respond.

Caution: Many companies have adopted the policy of cutting and pasting a canned response like: "We are sorry to hear that you were dissatisfied. Please call our store manager at…" This is not going to cut it. Customers know you put no effort into addressing that complaint especially when it's the same answer for every complaint that is posted. Here is a better action plan.

a. Acknowledge the complaint – Say something like, "We hear you! "or "I read your review today."

b. Apologize – This is not the forum to accept liability, but you should apologize that the customer's experience wasn't the best it could have been. Say something like, "Oh no, we hate to hear that you weren't happy" or "I'm so sorry we didn't meet your expectations this time."

c. Explain or offer – If you know what went wrong (even if it was the customer's unreasonable demand or a misunderstanding) explain it. Say something like, "It looks like the warranty for your freezer expired a month ago. But I'd love to talk to you about other alternatives to win your trust again." If you don't know what went wrong, offer to help. Say something like, "I want to personally help you resolve this issue, but I'm a bit unclear on some of the facts. Can you please call the store and ask for Lara. I have let my staff know to interrupt me wherever I am when you call." The goal is to move the complaint away from the public forum and put you back in control.

d. Compensate when appropriate – If your company really did the drop the ball or if there is something you can give the customer to appease them, make the offer. Say something like, "We always strive to make every customer happy. I'd love to have you come back so I can shake your hand, apologize again in person, and give you 20% off on your next visit."

Positive customer reviews are also incredibly important to your business. You should respond to them as well. The caution here is the same as above: no canned cut-and-paste responses. If someone has taken the time to tell you how awesome your company is, you should take the time to answer with a unique response. Keep it brief. This doesn't need to be a doctoral dissertation. Simply thank the customer for noticing how hard you work to make them happy.

According to research by Microsoft, "52% of people around the globe believe that companies need to take action on feedback provided by their customers." That alone emphasizes the importance of hearing a customer out. It's free advice that can help you recognize some blind spots and help you improve. Plus, if you're able to salvage that relationship in the process, it's a win/win/win.

In-person complaints are a retailer's gold mine, not an inconvenience. A person who takes the time to complain in person has done your company a great service. Companies pay consultants thousands of dollars to find weaknesses and deficiencies. Customers do it for free. No, customers actually <u>pay</u> you for the right to complain. They've plunked down their hard-earned money for a product or service, and now they are giving you valuable feedback about it. Their reports are not as sophisticated as a consultant might provide. But the consulting firm will not be able to provide the detail and passion the customer can give you.

Train your team members to handle in-person complains well.

1. Move the complaint away from earshot of other customers.

2. Ask for the customer's name and use it 2-3 times. Failure to use their names depersonalizes the interaction. Using the customer's name over and over is irritating and makes the customer think you are scripted, robotic, and/or condescending.

3. Team members should be trained to maintain strong eye contact while the customer is speaking.

4. Customers should NEVER be interrupted while voicing a complaint. An angry customer is a "tempest in a teapot." They need to release all of their steam before you can help them.

5. Team members should be trained to nod frequently while the customer is speaking. This signals engagement, listening, and concern.

6. Team members should restate the problem once the customer finishes. This serves two purposes: 1) It signals to the customer that you were paying attention and

understand their concern. 2) If you missed any salient points, it allows the customer to correct you.

Customers should never be told to "Calm down" when they are angry. That only makes them angrier. And the greatest cardinal sin is to say to a customer, "I'm sorry, there is nothing I can do." Instead, softly reassure the customer that you are there to help. "Please know that I am going to do everything I can to help you."

Summarize the issue after the conversation to confirm that you're both on the same page, and then move forward from there by trying to find a way to satisfy that customer's needs.

CASE STUDY: STATE FARM

State Farm is like any other insurance company in that their main business is fixing problems. But, it's the way in which they go about hearing out those problems that helps them stand out from competitors. Even State Farm's commercials make it clear that they go above and beyond to stand with customers through turmoil.

Their jingle in itself, "Like a good neighbor, State Farm is there," emphasizes their customer service policy of being there for you if you run into any problems.

Of course, knowing how to handle a customer complaint can always be tricky. Even if you can't instantly solve the issue, you can certainly express empathy for the customer. For instance, "I'm so sorry you're going through this," is one of the main sincere thoughts that State Farm agents try to express when people call with a claim.

In the State Farm Claims School training, new team members are taught to, "Put a smile in your voice." The theory is that customers can *hear* a smile as easily as they can see one. So, team members are encouraged to physically smile during phone contact to add that unseen element of friendliness.

Angie Demar recounted her experience working at State Farm.

> *Being a senior claims representative at State Farm was more about pleasing the customer than it was about the very important task of settling the claim. We were taught how to put the customer at ease and help them trust that we were going to take care of everything they bargained for when they bought their insurance from us. After all, they were contacting us after a catastrophic event in their lives: a car accident. They were suffering trauma. In many cases, they were still in shock from the crash, nursing their injuries, angry about being hit by a careless driver, or mourning the loss of a loved one who perished in the accident. If ever there was a time for the company to deliver the highest level of customer service, this was it.*

CHAPTER 8
PERSONALIZE CUSTOMER EXPERIENCES

Personalized customer experiences make customers feel special. It's truly that simple, but if you are about to overlook the power of personalization, just have a look at these statistics:

- "33% of customers who abandoned a business relationship last year did so because personalization was lacking."

- "72% of consumers say that when contacting customer service they expect the agent to know who they are, what they have purchased and have insights into their previous engagements."

So, ideally, when a customer walks into your store or calls up your hotline, your representatives should already know about them. That might seem impossible, but technology is making a lot easier. With the right CRM (Customer Relationship Management) system in place, your reps will be able to instantly pull up a customer's file.

This file will have all of their purchase history and previous service calls in one place so that representatives can easily catch up with where a customer is at when they need help. Maybe they have a question about a product, so all the rep has to do is look at their purchase history and see exactly which product they have in hand. Or, maybe they want to return or exchange a product, in which case the rep can instantly locate the order information and get that processed for them.

What's more, such a system allows each rep to add notes to the customer's file following the service call. This helps all other reps better serve the customer in future interactions with them.

Personalization means being able to know who your customer is and what they need from your business, and then offering them the products that best fit their lifestyle. This goes back to anticipating your customers' needs, but beyond narrowing products down to a particular segment of your audience, you are now getting personal at the individual level to truly speak to them about what they are buying and how your company can help them.

Personalized customer service is becoming more and more expected from companies. Apple is already way ahead of the game with the examples I gave earlier because they make the point of speaking to each customer and understanding what they want before they even think about showing products off.

It's customer service on steroids — knowing your customers and letting them know you know them. Local banks in small towns really get this right. Many of them greet their customers by name and know the details of their accounts. For that reason, they can make recommendations and stave off potential problems.

The 1980s television show, Cheers, coined the term, "where everybody knows your name." If you watched the show, you will remember the quintessential shout, "Norm!" whenever Norm Peterson came into the bar. We all want to have the "Norm" experience where the places we spend our money know us and ensure that our experience is tailor made for us.

> *"Remember that a person's name is, to that person, the sweetest and most important sound in any language."*
> —*Dale Carnegie,*
> *How to Win Friends and Influence People*

But it goes even farther. When interacting with customers, it is critical to listen to the customer to determine ways where the experience can be personalized. If a customer is shopping with a small child, offer a sweet treat or take them to the small desk with crayons by the register where kids can safely color while parents check out.

Trader Joe's team members are trained to listen and remember their customers. Imagine their delight when they enter the store and hear, "I remember you like seafood. We have a new shrimp scampi meal I think you'd like."

CASE STUDY: NORDSTROM

If you've never shopped at a Nordstrom before, let me go ahead and say that it's not like shopping at other retail stores. At Nordstrom, you are generally greeted within a few minutes of entering. That's because Nordstrom doesn't just want customers aimlessly browsing their stores or grabbing a bunch of items off the rack to see what works. Instead, Nordstrom team members act as "personal stylists" who will come up to you after you have found a couple things to look at and they will guide you to a fitting room where you can try things on.

During your visit at Nordstrom, you can look as much as you want and try on as much as you want, but if you're up for it, your "personal stylist" will be there to help. They're going to talk to you about what you are looking for. Maybe you're just browsing—in which case they're happy to check in with you every so often to see how you're doing, and otherwise let you look around and try things on as you wish. But, most often, people come into Nordstrom with a few specific things in mind.

Maybe you have entered wanting to get some new outfits for the new season or perhaps you really want a replicate a specific look or style. You just tell your stylist that and they will go all around the store trying to hunt down pieces you like that are in your size. While you're in the fitting room, they will check in on you as you try on different outfits. If you don't like something, easy: just hand it back to them and they'll run it back to the rack. If you want it in a different color, they'll go hunting for it. If they can't find it in a different color, they'll try to find something similar that you might like instead.

The point is, much like Apple, Nordstrom has trained its team members to get hands-on with each customer. They work to make an individualized and personalized experience that has you feeling like a VIP. The result is that many people I know will only shop at Nordstrom's because it's just so unlike (and above) any other retail clothing store at the same price point.

"We'd like to hire you for our Customer Service Department. It's practically impossible to look at a penguin and feel angry."

CHAPTER 9
ALWAYS FOLLOW UP

If you want your customers to remember you, you have to remember them. That means reaching out to your customers even, especially, when they haven't interacted with your company in a long time.

Following up with customers is actually one of the most important customer service activities you can commit to. Think about your recent brand interactions and you can likely think of a few follow-ups that you received in return.

The follow-up is especially important for companies that sell "big ticket" items. Think real estate agents and car dealerships. While you may think just the opposite, the fact is, these places need to follow-up more than anyone. Not just to make sure that the customer is happy with the experience they had, but also to stay at the forefront of the customer's mind.

While a real estate agent or a car dealership has a much longer sales cycle compared to a retail store or another type of company, these places know the follow-up is valuable because it will mean the difference between lots of referrals or no referrals at all.

Of course, follow-ups are important at every type of company. Whether you sell big-ticket items, small-ticket items, consumables, subscriptions, or something else, when you follow-up with a customer, you are opening the doors for their repeat business and also to the business of their friends and family.

There are many ways to follow-up. While one of the most common is through email, you can also follow-up through the mail. Think about sending birthday, anniversary, or special occasion cards to your most recent clients. Give them a call sometimes just for the sake of seeing how they like their new car or furniture or whatever it is you sold to them. When you begin making your customer service approach truly friendly, you'll likely end up becoming real friends with some of your best clients.

Wanda Bader of Strategize Your Success writes:

> *It is no secret that people lead busy lives and they cannot always remember to do all the things they want or need to do. Simply sending out a little email, reminding them that your business is still there may be all it takes to stimulate a sale. Following up with customers can also make them feel special and appreciated. Offering them a special customer appreciation sale is one way to do this. This can, again, be done through email*

*marketing. Another twist is to send your customer
an actual card in the mail.*

When should you stop following up?

When you're dead. Just kidding. The only time to stop following up is when the customer asks you to stop. Otherwise, a potential customer can remain on your contact sheet for years. Business is very much about timing. If you sell refrigerators, customers may not need you today. But eventually, every one of us will be in the market.

CASE STUDY: SWEETWATER

Sweetwater is a music and audio company that has long made waves for its approach to customer service. They pretty much valued it before anyone really recognized the "mainstream" marketing value of good customer experience, and they continue to do so to this day.

Aside from receiving a little bit of candy in every box, customers are also pleasantly surprised by the wonderful follow-up and involvement of customer service reps at the company. Every so often, anyone who has made a purchase from Sweetwater will get a call from their very own "specialist." This is the audio professional who was assigned to their customer profile at the time they first joined.

By giving each customer their own specific contact at the company, Sweetwater is able to deliver that personalized service discussed earlier. They are also able to offer unique follow-ups that really make customers feel like friends. You get to know your specialist and they get to know you. They also care to hear about your audio needs and what you're doing with your music and audio equipment as time goes on.

These specialists, similar to Apple's staff members, are always interested in helping you figure out which equipment will work best for your needs. They aren't just going to sell you the highest priced item they can find. And, if something doesn't work for you, they make returning or exchanging it very easy. Plus, they offer a lot of training and assistance after you purchase a product, so that you can really try it out and make sure it's the best thing for you.

CHAPTER 10
EMPOWER YOUR TEAM MEMBERS TO TAKE CARE OF CUSTOMERS

Team members are the lifeblood of any company. They answer calls, greet customers, and are the first face consumers see when they come into contact with your company. Unfortunately, they are also, usually, the lowest paid and lowest ranking of the staff. They have the least power and often, the least amount of information. So when a situation occurs, they either know they don't have the authority to address it or are afraid of the backlash if they make a mistake.

We've all been in a situation where we reach the register, a problem occurs, and a manager cannot be found either because he or she is not onsite or is busy attending to another matter. What are the customer and team member to do? Usually, there is an excruciating wait while the team member frantically searches for someone (anyone) to help them resolve it. While they do, the line gets longer and longer behind the customer who is having the problem. This makes the customer anxious and infuriates the line of waiting customers. The team member is equally frustrated because he feels all that anger being directed at him.

Let's calculate the cost of not empowering that team member to handle the problem.

Scenario: A customer sees a sign on the shelf indicating that a jar of honey is $1.00 off. So, she grabs the jar of honey positioned directly above the sign that is marked at the regular price of $9.99 expecting that, when she reached the register, she will pay $8.99. When the jar honey rings up for $9.99, and the customer informs the cashier of the mistake, one of two things can happen:

1. The cashier can change the price to $8.99 and continue with the customer's order, or,

2. The cashier can spend 1-2 minutes summoning a manager. The manager can spend 1-2 looking through the circular to determine whether the item is on sale. The manager can spend 2-3 walking back (or usually sending someone else back) to the section of the store to determine the correct price. The manager can then correct the price at the cost of about a minute. God forbid, the jar was placed in the wrong spot and there really is no discount. The manager can then advise the customer that they grabbed the wrong jar and give them a choice of paying full price for the jar they have or getting the brand that matches the sale price. That could be another 2-3 minutes to go back and get the correct jar. Here is the math:

- 10 minutes of team member's time at $9/hour = $1.50
- 7 minutes of the manager's time at approximately $15/hour = $1.75
- Irritated customer with the problem and irritated customers in the line = **PRICELESS**

A fair criticism of this approach is, "What if team members give away the store? I'll go out of business." That's a reasonable concern. The truth is, customers are not out to get something for nothing by-and-large. The majority of people just want a fair price and want what they believe they have been promised. Furthermore, every point-of-sale register system allows managers to track discounts and voids. If you set clear boundaries about when team members are authorized to resolve problems and how much authority they have, you can measure to ensure everyone is staying true to the parameters you set. You will find that team members discount far less than you might think they would.

CASE STUDY: DISNEY

It's really no surprise that the "Happiest Place on Earth" makes the book at least twice for their great customer service. Disney does their best to avoid any customer service problems within their parks by always being super proactive and involved with each customer's experience.

If you've never been, take my word for it. From the moment you enter the park, you can tell that the entire staff is laser-focused on making this the experience of a lifetime. Disney spares no expense or effort in creating the perfect customer experience.

> *With an average annual attendance of over 52 million visitors, Walt Disney World is the most visited vacation resort in the world. The amount of manpower, creativity, machinery, and technology involved in keeping Disney World humming and innovating is simply astounding.*
> —MAGIC GUIDES (DISNEY MAGAZINE)

The truth is, most people only go to Disney, on average, between one and two times in their lifetime. So, there is little margin for error. At Disney, you will not experience the disinterested ticket taker or disgruntled parking lot attendant. Every single person working there is highly invested in making sure your visit is memorable. No one is too busy to take the time to say hello and give you a genuine smile. When you enter a shop or restaurant, they greet you right away. If you are newly married, they'll give you a "Happily Ever After" button. They also pass out buttons for other special occasions, like birthdays.

They just have a way of keeping on top of things and making everyone feel special. But, in the event that something does go wrong (which is usually a very *little* thing relative to real life problems), they run to the rescue and do the best they can to turn the experience around before it turns into a bad memory for a family who's visiting the park.

What I like about Disney is that they empower their cast members to a great extent. Not only with excellent customer service training so they always know how to approach and handle customers—even irate ones—but also with other tools. For instance, Disney actually gives cast members a stipend. This stipend comes out of the park's wallet, but each team member is able to use at his or her own discretion to fix little problems throughout the day and make everyone's experience just a bit more magical.

So, if a kid's balloon floats away in the middle of the day, rather than watching them cry or making the parents buy another balloon, a Disney cast member can swoop in with a brand new one. As I said, a child losing a balloon is a relatively small problem compared to "real world" problems, but when you're trying to have a carefree day at Disney, these little things can really take away from the experience.

By giving their staff the opportunity to fix these things at their own discretion, without having to call a manager for approval, Disney is really empowering their staff to offer the best customer service possible.

After all, no one likes to hear: "I'll have to ask my manager," which is always followed by a frustrating wait. But what's really great is, at Disney, you ideally won't even get to the point where you find a staff member to complain to. Perhaps before you've even really processed things as your child begins to cry over their lost balloon, a cast member has already acted and replaced it for them. That's what makes the parks so magical.

"I was not rude to the customer. I said 'drop dead, PLEASE!'"

CHAPTER 11
INTERNAL CUSTOMER SERVICE

The Container Store had an innovative idea: a store of containers. Customers could find everything they needed for organization and storage. They could even design a custom closet solution. The company went public in October 2013 and its stock price quickly soared to $45/share. Today, you can buy a share for less than $5 at the time of this writing.

CEO Melissa Reiff sounded the customer service death toll in a D Magazine article:

> *Reiff says she wants to keep The Container Store's culture intact and keep the company at the top of the "best places to work" rankings. But she's also trying to redefine how The Container Store operates, how it competes, and how it will grow in a future that seems to be skewing toward*

digital commerce. So, she's making changes. A lot of changes. They include laying off people for the first time in the company's history.

Imagine the impact of this poor internal customer service on the team members that were terminated. She dispatched an army of 92 team members who were depending on the Container Store to support their families to now become volunteer ambassadors of malice, resentment, and revenge.

But it goes even farther. The effect of the layoffs on the remaining team members is not at all positive. Team members who are "spared" don't experience the sense of relief companies and their CEOs might expect. Instead, the firings inspire concerns about the long-term financial wellbeing of the company and the viability of their own careers with the company. They begin to wonder if they are going to fall prey in the next round of termination. They spend valuable work time worrying about what move to make, if any. Turnover spikes after a round of layoffs and team members' ability to deliver the brand of upbeat and engaged customer service is damaged.

According to the Harvard Business Review reports Anthony Nyberg and Charlie Trevor, layoffs deal a tremendous blow to the remaining team members and have a long list of deleterious effects:

> *"Evidence from several researchers suggests that downsizing dampens survivors' creativity — a potentially dangerous development for almost any company… Downsizing tends to disrupt social networks and information exchange within companies, adding to employees' negative feelings…*

> *Layoffs tend to increase employees' levels of stress,
> burnout, and insecurity and to decrease morale,
> job satisfaction, and trust. Such perceptual
> changes are linked to greater turnover, diminished
> willingness of employees to help one another, and
> poorer job and company performance. One study
> found that the anticipation of downsizing can
> have an even stronger effect than layoffs them-
> selves on employees' negative perceptions of their
> work environment."*

But there's even more. The public perception of the company after a massive layoff effort is also negative. Customers who hear about layoffs in a particular company receive the message that the company is in trouble. A decreased workforce cannot possibly result in increased service in the mind of a layperson. They lose faith in the company's ability to deliver on its promises.

When companies resort to sacrificing their team members to save themselves, they suffer both short-term and long-term effects that may outweigh the financial trauma they trying to avoid in the first place.

CEOs often don't help themselves by making public statements that highlight their lack of concern for the effects of their decision proving to the public what they already suspect: CEOs are out of touch with the working class. And they're probably right.

Reiff said on the conference call where she delivered the news:

> *"I'm not going to be cute with the words. You can
> call it restructuring, layoffs, position elimination,*

> *whatever you want to call it. What happened was that we'd changed the way we've been running our stores and we found 92 positions that we could eliminate due to our new efficiency. I had to make the decision to do that. I was afraid I was going to be called the hatchet lady."*

Contrast Reiff's management style with that of Honeywell CEO, David Cote. When he took the reigns of Honeywell in 2002, the company was struggling to recover from some serious economic challenges including a merger that didn't "merge," enormous write-offs and multiple missed earnings. CEOs were jumping ship after a year on the job in the face of such difficulties.

But Honeywell has always had customer service (both internal and external) firmly etched in its corporate culture. Cote knew he had to cut costs but did not want to sacrifice customer service. So, he devised an ingenious idea: team members were asked to take unpaid leaves, or furloughs, rather than suffer a termination.

Cote said:

> *… we opted for furloughs, for several reasons. Most managers underestimate how much dis-ruption layoffs create; they consume everyone in the organization for at least a year.*

The effect was remarkable. The company's profits grew strong and it held its margins. Turnover of team members was minimal, and the standard of customer service Honeywell has been known for remained intact.

Cote said:

> *...not everything is about money: People aren't mercenary, and they want to be part of something successful that is bigger than themselves. We'd had a good track record since 2002, we had a lot of employees who believed in what we were doing, and we communicated it clearly. People could see that things wouldn't stay awful forever, so they hung in.*

Company-wide layoffs are just one of the ways businesses both large and small shoot themselves in the proverbial foot when it comes to internal customer service. Other culprits include lack of team member engagement, toxic workplace culture, and substandard internal networking.

Corporate giant Enron collapsed in 2001 filing bankruptcy in one of the largest company failures of all time. Widespread accounting irregularities gave rise to the company's demise. But, insiders are vocal about deep issues that existed in the company long before investigators started combing through the books. In fact, company spokespeople admit to extensive issues in their corporate culture citing, among many reasons, the failure to maintain "adequate communication" in "organizational issues." Their internal customer service was suffering and contributed to the company's downfall.

It's all about communication. Departments need to talk to each other just like they need to talk to customers. Every team member in a business is a customer of every other team member.

So let's talk about the mechanics of effective communication. Communication needs to meet three criteria:

1. **It needs to travel both ways**. When communication only comes down the corporate ladder from "up above," the company suffers. Upper management loses out on the perspectives of the team members who know the most about the company — their front-line team members. Front line team members need to be able to send communication up the ladder as easily as it can come down.

2. **It needs to be timely and accurate**. Information shared too late is useless information and leads to team member frustration. Managers and business owners should carefully plan times to share information with their front-line team members so that they can deliver the appropriate customer service.

3. **It needs to be open**. This is a tough one because secret, closed-door meetings have become the norm in corporate culture. In truth, secret meetings are common in businesses of all sizes. But meetings are never as secret as the participants think they are. Information leaks out that is often incorrect, incomplete, or, at least, out of context. Some smart business owners have taken great strides to keep information open and honest. Some are completely radical about it, like CEO Ray Dalio of the investment firm, Bridgewater Associates.

Bridgewater Associates, the world's largest hedge fund, records every meeting that takes place in the company.

"My most important principle is that getting at the truth, whatever it may be, is essential for getting better. We get at truth through radical transparency and putting aside our ego barriers in order to explore our mistakes and personal weaknesses so that we can improve."

Sounds great, right? Well, this CEO puts his "video camera where his mouth is." Every meeting at Bridgewater is recorded, cataloged and made available to any and every team member. This is a radical approach to transparency, but it works. New team members can learn from the videotapes all about the company's plans and challenges directly from the decision-makers who participated in the meeting. Current team members can hear anything said about themselves or their departments.

It might seem somewhat Nixonian to tape every conversation, but in a culture where those recordings are open and available, it has an amazingly calming effect. Gone are the days, at least in this company, when a management team is planning to fire a team member and the team member has no idea of their imminent doom. Team members know well in advance of any disciplinary action if there are concerns about their performance at Bridgewater. In fact, he states that, with this system, managers are more likely to include the team member in the initial conversations about difficult topics since they know the team member will hear it eventually. This has almost eliminated the need to terminate anyone based on poor performance.

You certainly don't have to go to those lengths. But there are many steps you can take to improve communication at your company.

Communicate important information commensurate with the level of its importance.

If the communication is that there are bagels in the conference room, it can be sent one time. But if the communication is about a new product offering, it needs to be sent repeatedly in different formats and from different departments. Why? Departments will share and react to the communication based on its impact in their part of the company.

Allow departments to interface with each other about key issues.

This information sharing allows each department to understand and appreciate the impact of a decision on a neighboring department. The same is true for small companies. A change in the company of any importance is going to be felt and handled differently by each department.

For example, a company decides to decommission their work-from-home option for its 20-person sales team. This decision affects the office manager because he or she will need to find office/desk space for twenty people. Security is affected because of the number of people in the building and parking lot. Furthermore, the hours salespeople work are often far different from the hours worked by administrative staff, so security may need to make adjustments. This decision affects the accounting department who will need to keep a close eye on expense reports which should change drastically now that salespeople are not driving to appointments. The marketing team can certainly seize this opportunity to work more closely with sales to determine what methods are effective and to plan new marketing initiatives.

> Make sure team members know everything they need to know. Set them up for success by arming them with knowledge.

We have all been caught in the "I don't know vortex" where, as a customer (or new team member), we have asked a question, and no one seems to have the answer. Departments that don't talk to each risk alienating a customer who will only give us a short period of time to answer their questions before moving on to a competitor.

CASE STUDIES

Several companies have taken internal customer service very seriously. As a result, they continue to grow and thrive.

Credit Karma has established a wide-open door policy on every level all the way up to CEO Kenneth Lin. "I want employees to feel like this is a mission we're all in together. An open-door policy sets the tone for this. Whenever I'm in my office and available, I encourage anyone to come by and share their thoughts about how they feel Credit Karma is doing," Lin says. By keeping the lines of communication open to his team members, he is able to stay on top of what customers need and want.

Worldwide marketing automation company, HubSpot, have executives who have developed thick skins. Team members and customer can share any comments or concerns they have with the top brass without fear of retribution. Founder Dharmesh Shah instituted a practice called, "Ask Dharmesh Anything. As result, they heard from team members that they were "naïve" or "disconnected."

Social media manager, Buffer, has taken team member communication and engagement to the extreme. They have essentially outlawed privacy as it relates to corporate documents and emails. Emails are no longer private at Buffer. Everyone can see everything. When asked why, CEO Joel Gascoigne said, "transparency breeds trust, and trust is the foundation of great teamwork."

"We're seeing a significant drop in customer complaints since we stopped answering our phones."

CHAPTER 12
HAPPY TEAM MEMBERS
= HAPPY CUSTOMERS

Happy team members mean happy customers. Overly simplistic? No! In fact, it is unbelievably complex and rather difficult to maintain the corporate happiness factor especially as companies scale. Think back to the 60s and 70s. Most retail locations were storefronts owned by a single person or family. All of the team members were likely related to the owner. Calculate what the engagement of each team member might be at that time and how it might affect each customer as they entered the store. They would likely be greeted by the owner himself or herself receiving the highest level because that owner had the most to gain (or lose) by the level of customer service you received. But even if the owner was not present, it is likely a family member would be. That family member understood that their subsistence relied on their customer base. They were actively engaged in providing every customer with a quality shopping experience. Even if the store had grown to the point that a team member outside of the family needed to be hired, that team member understood the opportunity he or she had in working for the company. They knew that there were dozens of others who would kill for the job. And they were supervised, in most cases, directly by the owner. So, while that team member had the least invested in the success of the company, the level of customer service was still exceptionally high.

Imagine pulling up to such a store fifteen minutes after it had closed desperate to make a purchase. The owner would be locking the doors, but would gladly unlock them, turn the lights on, and complete your sale. Why? The owner was highly engaged with the satisfaction level of every customer. That sale was precious to him or her and the exceptional customer service would likely produce a repeat customer which is business gold!

Fast forward to today. The person delivering the customer service to the average customer is many degrees separated from the founder of the company and even farther removed the company profitability. The team member has, in most cases, never met the owner personally having only seen a 15-minute long video or him or her during their onboarding process back when they were a new hire. The owner's passion and vision are not likely to be paramount in the mind of the team member. They don't have a stake in the long-term success of the business. So, one customer doesn't matter much, or so they think.

A friend of mine once arrived at a Mexican restaurant 14 minutes before closing. She whipped her car into the parking space and sprinted toward the door filled with gratitude to the traffic fairies that she had made it there before closing. What she found is a perfect example of the state of modern customer service. The chairs were on top of the tables. The floor was wet. A mop and bucket sat in the center of the dining area. Half of the food had been removed from the warmers, and there was not a team member in sight. It was clear that, although it was not yet closing time, the team members' minds were closed to the idea of feeding one more customer. They were too far removed from the heartbeat of the company.

Was she greeted by cheerful team members ready to serve? On the contrary, she was met with frowns and angry stares. Her food was unceremoniously dumped into her bowl. No one said hello. No one said goodbye. And no one said thank you.

PRO TIP: Business owners who don't personally open and close their own stores should make it a habit to randomly arrive either a minute before closing or a minute before opening without warning to see what their customers are experiencing. You may be shocked to find your doors are already closed, the lights are off, and everyone has gone home.

Team members need to feel that they have a stake in the success of the company. How can this be done when team members are salary or hourly and will not benefit from any increase of profits the store enjoys?

There are several strategies business owners can employ to increase team member engagement that will have a direct effect on the team member's ability to deliver stellar customer service:

1. Know your team members.

    In a small company, this is as easy as scheduling quarterly gatherings where the entire company comes together. This is not a meeting. It's a gathering. It can be as simple as chips and dip, some music of the PA, and a game or two. It can last as little as an hour. The key is that you as the company owner are present. Team members need to see you behaving as a real person. They need to see you laugh. The need to see at a time when you are not talking about projections, sales, or quotas. You are the face of the company to them, so the gift of your time will be treasured by them.

    In a Forbes magazine article, Philip Dana of Bridgepoint said, "Breaking bread with your crew and listening to what's on the minds of those doing the bulk of the work is critical to establishing leadership presence. Don't order a sandwich so you can sit in your office. Go to the cafeteria and ask the loudest, most energetic table if you can join them for lunch. They're likely the influencers of your organization and would greatly appreciate your presence."

    In a mid-sized company with many locations, it becomes more difficult to find the time to visit each satellite. In that case, you may need to schedule once or twice-yearly gatherings at a venue. However, you will defeat your purpose if, at such an event, you take a microphone and offer a greeting and then disappear. You need to walk around and meet the people who make your machine run.

In a large company with several locations, your physical presence may be impossible. A CEO with 300+ stores and 2000+ team members stretched across many states can't visit them all in a year. And it becomes cost-prohibitive and logically impossible to get them all together in one space. This is where technology can assist. Virtual video conferences are a powerful way to have a <u>two-way</u> conversation with team members. Using this technology, it becomes quite easy to assemble up to 100 team members in a space so that you can see them, and they can see you. This is your opportunity to thank your team members for all they do and then allow them to speak while you listen to whatever it is they want to share with you.

Your middle managers can help you here. Did someone just have a new grandchild or send a teen off to college? Your managers can give you that information so that you can acknowledge that great achievement in the video conference. Imagine team member Wanda's surprise when you congratulate her on her recent wedding and tell her how jealous you are that she got to spend a week in Hawaii? After such an acknowledgement, Wanda no longer works for ABC Company — she works for you because you like her. And guess what? She likes you too. Her engagement skyrockets, and her customer service is elevated in the process.

Social media a great way to connect individually with team members. Business owners should comment at least weekly on their team members' positive posts. Imagine how Jack would feel if he posted on your company website "Celebrating my 25th Wedding Anniversary" and you as the company owner reply, "Save a slice of cake for me!" If social media is not a suitable way to connect, a simple card would do wonders.

2. Communicate your customer service vision clearly and often.

    Careershift.com reports that 61% of team members don't know their company values as it relates to customer service. A whopping 57% of team members who know it find it unappealing, unintelligible, or unmotivating. That's a problem! Your company's mission statement should clearly identify the value you bring as an organization to your customers. It should be concise and catchy. Once it is whittled down to the bare bones, it should be posted everywhere for team members (and customers) to easily and frequently see. It should be a part of every corporate conversation. It should be on all corporate documents, communications, and merchandising. In that way, customer service becomes more than just a byword, it gets ingrained in the DNA of your culture.

3. Establish an open-door policy.

    Team members who feel free to voice ideas and concerns in the workplace are highly engaged in the success of the company. When a team member's grievances are heard and addressed, they experience a feeling of comfort and safety in the workplace. When they propose an idea and see it implemented, they are overcome with euphoria. They know that they matter to the company which inspires more ideas. Even if the idea isn't a good one, the team member should be praised for taking the initiative to share and encouraged to keep the ideas coming. The important thing is that they are being heard which staves off team member dissatisfaction.

4. Reward, reward, reward.

Business owners take a huge risk when they open their companies. They often put their own money, their credit, and other assets on the line. They pour their blood, sweat, and tears into the success of the company. And they spent countless hours preparing for the grand opening only to increase the number of hours they have to invest after the company launches. It's your baby. The payoff is that, if all goes well, you reap profits, recognition, and a sense of accomplishment when the company flourishes. Your team member has done none of that. In fact, all they have invested in the time it took to complete their job applications. They are merely trading time for dollars. And, sadly, most team members work just hard enough not to get fired because they think you are paying them just enough so that they don't quit. You can reverse this vicious cycle by establishing a culture where team members are highly rewarded for delivering the highest level of customer service they are capable of.

a. Set up a reward system where team members get points for positive customer reviews both online and in-person. The top ten point-getters in a month should receive a prize. Some business owners give gifts. Others give cash rewards. One ingenious business owner gave a day-off with pay for the top three people that month. Team members love it!

b. Read EVERY positive review to the entire team. It has been wisely said that "People will work for money, but they will die for recognition." Without fail, you should publicly acknowledge each and every note or word of praise and gratitude you receive from customers. This creates another cycle — a very positive and powerful one — where team members strive to be mentioned among those who gave exceptional customer service.

c. Remind your team members (and yourself) that they are the "secret sauce" of your business. In case you haven't yet figured it out, they are! Business is about two things: people and products/services. Without your staff, your business will crash and burn. It helps to let people know how much you appreciate that, although they could work for some other company, they choose to work here. When team members work late or come in early, acknowledge it. When team members go the extra mile or perform services outside of their job descriptions, make a big deal of it. When employers praise positive performance, they will get much more of the same.

d. Compensate fairly. This is a sticky subject. But no discussion of satisfying your internal customers (your team members) would be complete without highlighting the foolish practice of underpaying team members. We live in the information age. That means that it's harder than ever to keep secrets. It is very likely that your team members know what everyone else in your company is earning. And they know what their counterparts in your industry are earning. Unless you are at the top of that heap, your team members are always wondering if they can make more money doing the same job somewhere else. You should be making every effort to compensate as fairly as you can, or your company will be a continual revolving door. The cost of "on-boarding" a new team member far outweighs a $.50 or $1.00 per hour wage increase. Studies by both Glassdoor.com and the Society for Human Resource Management cites that the average cost to recruit, hire and train a new team member is at around $4,000. Do the math. As the old saying goes, "It's cheaper to keep her!" This cost doesn't factor in the full cost of bringing someone up full speed.

e.   Plan for raises – After many years as an entrepreneur and business adviser, I am still surprised by managers who are surprised when team members ask for raises. It is inevitable. So, build it into your hiring plan from the beginning. When team members ask for a raise or are scheduled for a review, you will be prepared to increase their salaries appropriately. If a team member is not eligible for an increase, outline to him or her exactly what must be done and provide a definitive date on their reevaluation.

For example: Let's assume Jeff sells piping to local manufacturers and he is up for his one-year evaluation. By now, you should have had multiple conversations with Jeff about his work. The review is your opportunity to detail, in writing, where his performance is missing the mark. Say to him, "Jeff, you are a valuable team member and we want to continue our relationship with you. You're doing a great job. We would love to increase your pay. However, there are two areas where I need to see improvement. 1) You would need to upsell your orders by 10%. 2) You would need to increase your customer feedback score by 10 points. Jeff, in 45 days, we will meet again and see if you have met those goals. If you have, I will increase your commission by 5%.

PRO TIP: Review Jeff's performance in 30 days. If he has met the goal, surprise him with the raise two weeks early. You will shoot his loyalty, morale, and performance through the roof.

Ralph Waldo Emerson said, "Happiness is a perfume you cannot pour on others without getting a few drops on yourself."

The toxic workplace environment is probably the number one killer of good customer service. When team members dislike and distrust one another, it is difficult for them to be open and positive with customers.

A toxic workplace environment is easy to spot. Team members don't smile when customers approach them. They don't greet customers (or each other) when they walk by. Sometimes, real-live team member-to-team member or team member-to-supervisor battles take place. Those public battles are usually loud and occasionally physical. The result? Customers who witness them silently vote no to patronizing that business ever again.

Business owners often see these conflicts as a sign of unprofessionalism. They are wrong. While unprofessionalism is a growing concern in our "me-focused" society, these conflicts are actually the result of toxicity in the workplace environment. Thinking that team members who are behaving badly are simply unprofessional and need to be fired is the same as thinking that a fish tank whose walls are green with algae, dense with waste, and full of dead fish will be treated by tossing the dead fish and dropping in new ones.

If your workplace environment is toxic, it doesn't matter the caliber of team member you hire, they will be contaminated by the environment in which they are placed. They may begin their employ eager, enthusiastic, energetic, and strait-laced, but they will soon begin to falter and behave much like those around them if only for survival's sake.

Symptoms of a toxic workplace culture:
* Excessive lateness, early departure or absenteeism
* Gossiping
* Absence of pleasantries among team members or from team members to customers
* Accusations of favoritism

Let's follow the fish tank analogy a little further. People who place goldfish (or nearly any other fish) in a fishbowl often think that it is normal for their fish to live about a year and grow to be a few inches long. They don't realize the tragic mistake they are making.

Goldfish, when placed in the right environment, can easily live up to ten years. A few have made it to twenty. What's more astonishing is that the goldfish you see in the pet store are babies in the truest sense of the word. In the right medium, that tiny goldfish can grow to more than a foot long. They stay small and die young all because of the environment in which they are placed.

The same is true for your team members. In a poisonous, unhealthy, and contaminated environment, no great team member can thrive.

The cure? Immediately begin the conversation about workplace culture. Take responsibility (since it is your responsibility) for the poor environment and personally commit to making it better.

Never engage in toxic behaviors yourself. For example, when you talk badly about one team member to another, you communicate to the team member with whom you are speaking that you are as likely to trash them behind their backs.

Bring Back the Pleasantries

Greet every team member when you see them and throughout the day. Say "Please" and "Thank you" with every request. Talk about how important it is to "ask" for what you want rather than command someone to do what you want.

Increase Attendance

As the leader, you should show up early and leave late. When you are chronically absent, your team members will be as well because you have set that as the tone. Once you demonstrate that you are committed to being present, you can set that as the standard for your team members.

Establish a Zero-Tolerance Policy for Gossip

Never entertain gossip from anyone. Even your closest friends at work should be discouraged from gossip. It tears at the fabric of morale for both the gossiper and gossip.

Treat Chronic Lateness like a Symptom

If team members are chronically later, treat it clinically. Sit with the team member and ask the reasons for the recurrent lateness. This places them on notice that you are aware of the problem and gives them an opportunity to brainstorm with you ways to address the lateness. Perhaps the team member's work schedule (that you planned) is not conducive to their lifestyles.

Take Katie for example. She is scheduled to work from 8 – 4. However, she drops her daughter off at the bus stop at 7:40 and then drives fifteen minutes to work in the opposite direction. If the bus is more than five minutes late (which it often is), Katie will be late to work. If Katie is an otherwise stellar team member, a focused manager would alter her schedule to 8:15 – 2:15 allowing her the flexibility to meet her responsibilities at home and at work. She even has time to swing into Starbucks for a coffee. Imagine how her productivity and responsiveness to customers would soar.

In a NY Times article, Simon Slade wrote:

> *Nothing telegraphs how much you trust your employees than the freedom to set their own hours. And that's exactly what I do in my own company… my employees have flexible work hours, all year long. David G. Javitch, an organizational psychologist, leadership specialist and president of Javitch Associates in Newton, Mass., [writes] 'employees can choose to come into [our] office any time from 7 am to 7 pm as opposed to the traditional 9 to 5, or [they can] work 40 hours in four days instead of five.' I take it even further. My employees have complete control over their [work] schedules."*

Both of these CEO innovators value the performance and customer satisfaction rates of these team members over and above hours on a time clock. The result is that the team member is more engaged when interfacing with customers. Customer responses are overwhelmingly positive.

COACH TEAM MEMBERS TO RESOLVE THEIR OWN CONFLICTS

Whenever team members develop their problem-solving skills, everyone wins: the company, the team member, and the customer. As Jayson DeMers states in an entrepreneur.com article:

> *As an entrepreneur, you're the visionary and leader of your company, but your employees are the ones who will carry your business to success. They're carrying out your vision, working with your customers, and coming up with ideas of their own when need be.*
>
> *The better they are at their jobs, the more likely your business is to succeed, but one of the most important qualities for a worker is also one of the most elusive: the ability to solve problems efficiently.*
>
> *Problem-solving can't be taught the way algebra, basic work duties or software can. It requires more creativity and abstract thinking, as well as an ability to remain calm under pressure and see the bigger picture.*

CONCLUSION

Today's customer is more savvy, connected, and vocal than any customer at any time in history. They have a plethora of choices, they can price shop in a matter of seconds, and if you fail them, they will walk—but not before telling everyone they know (and many more they don't know). Customers expect quality products and great prices. But they will not forgive shoddy customer service to get them.

> *"You'll never have a product or price advantage again. They can be duplicated easily, but a strong customer service culture can't be copied."*
> —*Jerry Fritz,*
> *Director of Management Institute,*
> *University of Wisconsin*

> *It takes months to find a customer and seconds to lose one.*
> —*Vince Lombardi,*
> *NFL Executive*

Do what you do so well that they will want to see it again and bring their friends."

— WALT DISNEY

These may sound like clichés, but they are so much more. They are the foundation and basis for successful business. Customer service requires laser-focus on the most important element of our business: the purchaser of the product or service we offer. Servicing them means serving them — listening to their needs, anticipating their desires, and making sure that your team members share in your passion to keep the customer first.

"Good customer service is rare. When something is
rare, it is valuable. When something is valuable,
it is expensive. Bad customer service is our
way of helping our customers save money!"

John 3:16

HIRING MIKE TO SPEAK

Well, hello! If you are an event planner (or know someone who is), let's have a conversation. I'd love to bring my message of hope to your corporation, conference, business, or church. Since I do this for a living, I can't do it for free, but if you have a budget or want to talk about raising up a budget to bring me in, reach out to me!

www.mikejtoy.com

ONLINE TRAINING

Did you find this book helpful? If so, consider diving even deeper with our learn-at-your-own-pace courses. The content is more advanced and doesn't overlap with the book much so you'll learn even more new ideas and concepts. Just one application can easily pay for itself. Perfect for individuals or organizations.

www.mikejtoy.com

HIRING MIKE TO BE YOUR ADVISOR

One of the fastest ways of growing your business or company is to tap into someone who is both knowledgeable and skilled at both identifying your areas of opportunity and providing wise counsel.

I'm not for everyone because I'm super expensive, but for the right business I can help you cut expenses while boosting your income. My services will pay for itself several times over.

Some of the areas we can work together on include:
- Operations
- Hiring
- Marketing
- Traffic (Not the kind where there are lots of cars)
- Leadership
- Communication
- Systems
- Positioning
- Website Design
- Speaking
- Sales
- Customer Service

- Management
- Branding
- Training

These are just a few areas listed. If you're interested in learning more, please reach out!

www.mikejtoy.com

SOCIAL MEDIA

Follow me on social media! I'll have exclusive content you won't find anywhere else.

Facebook: www.mikejtoy.com/fb

Twitter: www.mikejtoy.com/tw

LinkedIn: www.mikejtoy.com/in

Instagram: www.mikejtoy.com/ig

YouTube: www.mikejtoy.com/yt

OTHER BOOKS BY MIKE TOY

The Magic of Influence
How to Get Anyone to Do Anything

The Magic of Customer Service
How the Best Companies Keep Everybody Happy

The Magic of Culture
Secrets of Highly Productive Teams

The Magic of Leadership
How to Get People to Follow You

The Magic of Management
How to Bring Out the Best From Others

The Magic of Sales
How to Sell Anyone Anything

The Magic of Persuasion
How to Win Others Over Without Twisting Their Arms

It's Not Magic
Secrets of Performing at Your Best

To purchase bulk copies of any of his
books for your customers or organization,
please contact www.mikejtoy.com

ABOUT THE AUTHOR

Mike Toy is someone who just can't sit around and do nothing. In fact, he wants a piece of every action. When Mike was just seven years old he announced to the world that he was going to become both an astronaut and the President of the United States one day.

Mike's extensive background as a comedy magician and keynote presenter had him speaking for Fortune 500 companies. He has appeared on ABC, NBC, CBS, and FOX. Mike's TEDx Talk is one of the most unique presentations people have ever seen (That's what he said!). And one of his highlights was being invited to speak by The White House.

Mike graduated from the University of California, Davis in 2001 with a degree in human development. He picked that major because it was the easiest program available. Mike was able to get decent grades without doing a whole lot of work because for projects he recruited the smartest students to be in his group. He was the recipient of the UC Davis Community Service Award for his ground breaking method in helping low-achieving high school students reach their potential.

To make up for slacking academically in college, Mike graduated with a Masters in English from San Francisco State University in 2011. This tells you that he is cultured, can quote Shakespeare in his sleep, and is cool. His interest in helping people spiritually led him to taking courses at The Cornerstone Seminary and The Master's University.

Determined to help people realize their dreams, Mike picked up business skills and knowledge. He's a graduate of Seth Godin's altMBA, where he grew fond of the term "ruckus-maker". Mike's interest in marketing led him through Donald Miller's Storybrand certified guide program. One of his favorite books is Dale Carnegie's classic "How to Win Friends and Influence People", which led him to become one of their trainers.

He was born and raised in San Francisco. In his free time, he enjoys beach volleyball and Korean bbq galbi (short ribs). Mike loves traveling to Asia with his church to serve the underprivileged and orphans. His Chinese mom is praying he would find his wife soon.

URGENT PLEA!

Thank You for Reading My Book!

I really appreciate all of your feedback, and
I love hearing what you have to say.

I need your input to make the next version of
this book and my future books better.

Please leave me a helpful review on Amazon letting
me know what you thought of the book.

Thanks so much!!

Mike Toy

FREE BONUS

You've made a wonderful choice to pick up this book. Because of this I want to provide you extra resources, insights, and surprises as you journey to becoming the best version of yourself possible.

Just go here…

www.mikejtoy.com/freebook

Nothing excites me more than your success. Looking forward to connecting with you!